Investigations

Pulling

Patricia Whitehouse

Heinemann Library
Chicago, Illinois

Designed by Sue Emerson, Heinemann Library; Page layout by Que-Net Media
Printed and bound in the United States by Lake Book Manufacturing, Inc.
Photo research by Beth Chisholm

07 06 05 04 03
10 9 8 7 6 5 4 3 2 1

Library of Congress Cataloging-in-Publication Data
Whitehouse, Patricia, 1958-
  Pulling / Patricia Whitehouse.
      p. cm. – (Investigations)
Includes index.
Summary: Presents simple hands-on experiments that demonstrate what can make pulling easier or more difficult.
  ISBN 1-4034-0909-9 (HC), 1-4034-3468-9 (Pbk.)
  1. Force and energy--Juvenile literature. 2. Power (Mechanics)–Juvenile literature. 3. Force and energy–Experiments–Juvenile literature. 4. Power (Mechanics)–Experiments–Juvenile literature. [1. Force and energy–Experiments. 2. Power (Mechanics)–Experiments. 3. Experiments.] I. Title.
  QC73.4 .W474 2003
  531'.6–dc21

                          2002014423

Acknowledgments
The author and publishers are grateful to the following for permission to reproduce copyright material:
pp. 4, 6, 7, 8, 9, 10, 11, 12, 13, 14, 15, 16, 17, 22, 23, 24, back cover Que-Net/Heinemann Library; p. 5 Ariel Skelley/Corbis; pp. 18, 19, 20, 21 Robert Lifson/Heinemann Library

Cover photograph by Que-Net/Heinemann Library

Every effort has been made to contact copyright holders of any material reproduced in this book. Any omissions will be rectified in subsequent printings if notice is given to the publisher.

Special thanks to our advisory panel for their help in the preparation of this book:

Alice Bethke,
Library Consultant
Palo Alto, CA

Eileen Day,
Preschool Teacher
Chicago, IL

Kathleen Gilbert,
Second Grade Teacher
Round Rock, TX

Sandra Gilbert,
Library Media Specialist
Fiest Elementary School
Houston, TX

Jan Gobeille, Kindergarten Teacher
Garfield Elementary
Oakland, CA

Angela Leeper,
Educational Consultant
North Carolina Department
of Public Instruction
Wake Forest, NC

Some words are shown in bold, **like this.**
You can find them in the picture glossary on page 23.

Contents

What Is Pulling?

Pulling is one way to move something toward you.

You can pull your toy to move it.

Some things are easy to pull.

Other things are hard to pull.

How Can You Pull Something Heavy?

This toy box is full.

You need to pull it away from the wall.

Try to pull the toy box with your hands.

Is it easy to do?

Now put a **handle** on the toy box.

What will happen when you pull on the handle?

A handle makes things easier to pull.

How Hard Do You Have to Pull?

This box is full of blocks.

You need to take it to another room.

Try to pull the box.

You have to pull hard to move the box over the **rough** carpet.

Now the box is on the
smooth floor.

Will you have to pull hard now?

You only have to pull a little bit.

The box is easier to pull on a smooth floor.

Can You Pull Something Heavier Than You?

This box of books is heavy.

How can you move it?

Tie a **handle** to the box.

It is too heavy to pull.

Ask a friend to help you.

Will you be able to pull the box now?

More people means more pull power.

You can pull the box together!

Can You Pull Down to Pull Something Up?

Your friend is on top of the bridge.

Can you get her something to eat?

You can tie a rope to a basket of fruit.

But how can the rope help?

Throw one end of the rope over the bar.

Now, pull down gently on the rope.

When you pull down, the basket goes up.

Your friend can grab a piece of fruit.

Quiz

Will the toy be easier to pull through the **rough** grass or over the **smooth** sidewalk?

Look for the answer on page 24.

22

Picture Glossary

handle
pages 8, 9, 15

rough
pages 11, 22

smooth
pages 12, 13, 22

Note to Parents and Teachers

In physics, force is defined as a push or a pull. This book offers children an opportunity to explore the physical laws of pulling in terms they can understand. Simple experiments demonstrate that the amount of force needed to pull an object depends on the size of the object and the surface it moves along. Children will also find out that pulling can change direction, which is the basis for understanding how pulleys work.

Read the first two pages of each chapter, and help children think of a solution to the chapter's question. For example, after reading pages 6 and 7, have the children try to pull a heavy box with their hands and then with a handle. Ask the children to think of objects that are pulled with a handle and whether they think using a handle makes the object easier to pull. Then read pages 8 and 9 and discuss whether your solution matched the one in the book or how it was different.

! CAUTION: Children should not attempt any experiment without an adult's permission and help.

Index

Answer to quiz on page 22

The toy is easier to pull on a **smooth** sidewalk.